GW00494366

THE

CHILDREN'S

ROOM

TRADITIONAL
WOODWORKING

THE

CHILDREN'S

ROOM

Step-by-step projects for the woodworker

COLLINS & BROWN

Copyright © 1998 Collins & Brown Limited

Text copyright © 1998 Collins & Brown Limited, *Traditional Woodworking* magazine

Illustrations copyright © 1998 Collins & Brown Limited, *Traditional Woodworking* magazine

Published by Collins & Brown Ltd,

London House, Great Eastern Wharf,

Parkgate Road, London SW11 4NQ

1 3 5 7 9 8 6 4 2

British Library Cataloguing-in-Publication Data:
A catalogue record for this book is available from the British Library.

ISBN 1 85585 473 2

A NOTE ON SAFETY

While the publishers can take no responsibility for the safety of any child
using or playing with the projects presented here, we do advise the following safety precautions:
• Make sure that all nails, woodscrews or other fittings are secure to avoid the danger
of a child swallowing such items or being otherwise injured by them.
• Take extra care when finishing to avoid rough edges.
• Always use child-safe paints (see p. 72).
• Always protect children from wood dust and any potentially.
dangerous tools or materials you use when working.

Please also note that, for the purposes of visual clarity in step-by-step photographs,
safety guards on power tools have at times been removed.
Always refer to the manufacturer's safety instructions
when working with any power or machine tool.

Series Editor: Liz Dean

Project Editor: Ian Kearey

Editorial Assistant: Lisa Balkwill

Designer: Alison Verity

Original design: Suzanne Metcalfe-Megginson

Illustrator: Keith Field

Editorial Director: Sarah Hoggett

Art Director: Roger Bristow

Printed in China

CONTENTS

INTRODUCTION

TRADITIONAL WOODWORKING magazine was launched in April 1988, its aim to give the amateur woodworker the opportunity to make high-quality furniture. Many years on, we are still bringing our readers features on the very latest woodworking techniques, testing new tools, and keeping them in touch with the latest developments. In addition, each month there are at least four beautifully designed projects to make. The best of these have been chosen for this series of books.

The furniture makers who designed and created these projects are long-standing contributors to *Traditional Woodworking*. They have been selected for their classic designs, high-quality craftsmanship and, not least, the ability to explain precisely how their pieces can be made. Making furniture and other items that will be used by children presents a different challenge; the pieces are more likely to take a few hard knocks in everyday use, and so the materials may be chosen specifically for strength and durability, rather than for colour or a fine figure. Yet this need not be a disadvantage, as it allows you to consider alternative coverings, to match bright existing furnishings, or to make the piece into a colourful focus. The Playhouse (p. 24) is large enough to become centrepieces in this way, while the Animal Safari (p. 10) and Character Mobile (p. 68) require more intricate paintwork.

Tools and Materials

The majority of these projects require less finely detailed work than those for the living room or dining room, yet a good basic set of hand tools, well sharpened and maintained, is essential. Power tools, such as a drill, jigsaw, router and sander, are useful for the more tedious jobs involved. In addition, a small powered fretsaw or jigsaw will prove invaluable when cutting out the shapes for the Teddy Bear Book Ends (p. 36), Caterpillar Peg Rail (p. 64), Animal Safari (p. 10) and Character Mobile (p. 68). However, most of the projects here can be made using hand tools only.

A basic hand-tool kit should consist of a workbench, G- and sash cramps, a selection of saws – tenon, coping, dovetail and ripsaw – and marking tools such as try squares, steel rules, mortise gauge, marking knife and a pencil. A hammer, mallet and drill are essential, as are planes, chisels, screwdrivers and some means of sharpening them. Don't forget a selection of sandpapers, graded from fine to coarse.

The projects in this book are made from solid softwood or hardwood – either commonly available native or imported timber – MDF or plywood. Alternative materials are suggested, so that you can make a choice of what to use, based on your preferences, the style of the piece, and how much you wish to spend. It is best to purchase wood from a local timber yard, rather than a home-improvement store: the choice of woods will be greater, and the yard will often cut the timber to meet the specifications – particularly useful when starting on a large project such as the Playhouse. On a project like the Rocking Horse (p. 16), consider what wood you will use before purchasing – a little extra money spent on wood with an attractive colour or figure could certainly make the project into a real eye-catcher.

Finishing and Decoration

In all the projects, you have the choice of following the instructions and advice given for that piece, or you can devise your own colour scheme or method of finishing. Whatever you choose, it is wise to be aware of the safety factor when choosing paints, and so there is a section at the back of the book on purchasing child-safe and non-toxic paints (pp. 72–73). Freehand painting, découpage and stencilling are also popular techniques

LEFT: *These colourful teddy bear book ends (p. 36) are easy to construct and can be made with plywood offcuts.*

RIGHT: *The basic design for the Toy Truck (p. 30) can be adapted for both younger and older children.*

for decorating children's furniture, so a section on stencilling and a stencil alphabet have been included (pp. 74–75),to give you a start; and there's no reason why you can't use any of the finishing techniques presented here on other projects.

Above all, we hope that you will enjoy making the projects in this book, from large to small, and that the children for whom they are made will get many years of pleasure from owning and using them.

Helen Adkins, EDITOR
Traditional Woodworking Magazine

ANIMAL SAFARI

*These toy wild animals, easily constructed
from various thicknesses of birch plywood,
are as popular with today's children as they have
been for hundreds of years. You could make
two of each to start a Noah's Ark collection.*

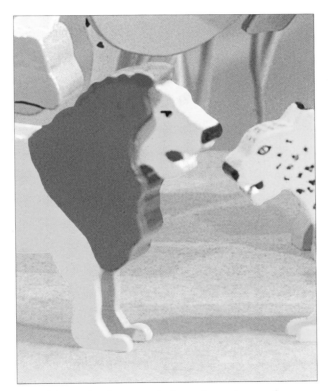

Most animals are made from three pieces only.

11

1 Transfer the middle section of each animal onto the relevant thickness of plywood, either by tracing or as here, by sticking photocopies onto the wood. You can photocopy the animals to different sizes if you prefer. Use a low-tack adhesive for this – a glue stick works well – so that the edges do not lift during fretsawing and the paper can be sanded away easily. Repeat the process for the outer side profiles of each animal and the elephant's ears and the ostrich's wings. Pin each thin piece of plywood onto another of the same thickness, so that you can cut both sides out together, to ensure an identical profile.

2 Cut out the shapes using a fretsaw; if you use a hand-held one, make sure that the blade does not become angled during cutting. Again, hand-fretsawing thicknesses over 12 mm ($\frac{1}{2}$ in) is not advised, so cut out the outer side sections of the elephant and rhinoceros individually. Sand off the glued paper from the middle sections.

Rhinoceros middle

3 Unpin all the pinned sections, sand off the paper, and glue each middle and side section together in the correct order – do not stick the elephant's ears or the ostrich's wings at this stage. PVA, or white woodworking glue, works well, because it allows you to manipulate the sections into place. Clamp each animal in a vice for a few minutes, then remove and allow to set overnight.

ANIMAL TEMPLATES *(shown about half actual size)*

OSTRICH BASE

4 When the glue has set, fill the pinholes with filler and clean up any uneven edges with sanding sticks and small files, making any necessary adjustments to the profiles.

5 Glue the elephant's ears and the ostrich's wings in place, clamp and allow to dry as before. You can now round and generally shape the edges of each animal to suit your requirements – for realism, the lion's mane can be left quite rough.

6 For the ostrich's base, mark a 35 mm (1⅜ in) diameter circle onto 4 mm (⅛ in) scrap plywood and cut it out with a fretsaw. Position the ostrich centrally on the base and mark around the tenon base of each foot. Fretsaw out the 'mortises' and glue the ostrich to the base.

7 Prime and paint the animals – you can either paint them with lifelike colours and details, or use a basic, bright and simplistic colour scheme. Enamel gloss paints are the best choice, being hardwearing and quite easily mixed.

Choosing Colours

The following colours were used for the animals shown in this project, and represent a basic selection that can be applied directly onto the animals, or mixed to make more subtle shades.

Light buff was used for the base colour of the lion and giraffe; tan for the lion's mane and tail hair; mid-brown for the giraffe's patches and hair; bright red for the inside of the lion's and leopard's mouths; black for the eyes, the zebra's stripes, the leopard's spots, the ostrich's feathers and general detailing; white for the base colour of the zebra, the ostrich's feathers and general detailing; pale grey for the base colour of the elephant and rhinoceros, and the zebra's and giraffe's hooves; and yellow for the ostrich's beak and the base colour of the leopard. The ostrich's neck and legs were decorated using a mixture of white, red and yellow.

LIST OF MATERIALS *(measurements indicate cut size)*		
ITEM	**SECTION**	**LENGTH**
GIRAFFE		
Plywood for middle, 1	145 x 12 mm (5¾ x ½ in)	233 mm (9⅛ in)
Plywood for sides, 2	160 x 6 mm (6¼ x ¼ in)	356 mm (1 ft 2 in)
LION		
Plywood for middle, 1	50 x 10 mm (2 x ⅜ in)	120 mm (4¾ in)
Plywood for sides, 2	70 x 4 mm (2¾ x ⅛ in)	160 mm (6¼ in)
LEOPARD		
Plywood for middle, 1	55 x 6 mm (2¼ x ¼ in)	110 mm (4¼ in)
Plywood for sides, 2	60 x 4 mm (2¾ x ⅛ in)	160 mm (6¼ in)
ZEBRA		
Plywood for middle, 1	75 x 12 mm (3 x ½ in)	120 mm (4¾ in)
Plywood for sides, 2	100 x 4 mm (4 x ⅛ in)	210 mm (8¼ in)
RHINOCEROS		
Plywood for middle, 1	70 x 6 mm (2¾ x ¼ in)	165 mm (6½ in)
Plywood for sides, 2	93 x 10 mm (3⅝ x ⅜ in)	305 mm (1 ft)
ELEPHANT		
Plywood for middle, 1	95 x 6 mm (3¾ x ¼ in)	220 mm (8¾ in)
Plywood for sides, 2	120 x 12 mm (4¾ x ½ in)	320 mm (1 ft ½ in)
Plywood for ears, 2	32 x 4 mm (1¼ x ⅛ in)	90 mm (3½ in)
OSTRICH		
Plywood for middle, 1	65 x 6 mm (2½ x ¼ in)	75 mm (3 in)
Plywood for sides, 2	60 x 4 mm (2⅜ x ⅛ in)	140 mm (5½ in)
Plywood for wings, 2	21 x 4 mm (⅞ x ⅛ in)	65 mm (2½ in)
Plywood for base, 1	35 mm (1⅜ in) diameter	4 mm (⅛ in)

ROCKING HORSE

This simple rocking horse, made from
well-seasoned pine, involves no carving
or complicated joints and is glued and screwed
together. The solid traditional safety stand
provides a proper swinging action,
to satisfy the most active riders.

The swing-irons are held on by brass brackets.

1 The head can be prepared from two pieces, each 146 mm (5¾ in) wide. Glue and clamp together the pieces to make up the head, and when dry, cut to 356 mm (1 ft 2 in) length. Mark out the profile of the head and neck, and cut out a bandsaw makes this job easier. Round over the edges of the head and neck, using a router with a rounding-over cutter: do not round over the base that fits along the seat, the front edges of the ears, the inside of the mouth and the nostrils. You can use a spokeshave, a chisel, or a lot of sanding to round over. Mark and drill a 19 mm (¾ in) hole through the neck for the handle. Cut the handle to 200 mm (8 in) length and glue in place. Mark and drill shallow holes for the eyes.

2 Mark and cut the seat to 535 mm (1 ft 9 in) length, and round over the edges, except where the head and rump join it. Mark and cut the rump and seat back to 125 mm (5 in) each, and drill a 19 mm (¾ in) hole in the back of the rump for the tail. Mark and drill pilot holes through the seat for the head and seat back, and through the seat back for the rump. Bevel the bottom of the seat back to fit against the rump. Glue and screw the head and seat back to the seat, and the rump to the seat back, each time recessing the screw heads.

3 Cut the legs to 460 mm (1 ft 6 in), and shape the profiles with a bandsaw, then cut the leg blocks to 125 mm (5 in). Mark and shape a 10 bevel on the top of the legs and the sides of the leg blocks. Glue and screw the legs to the leg blocks, checking the angle, then drill pilot holes through the leg blocks and glue and screw them to the underside of the seat.

4 Mark and cut the plywood body sides to 267 mm (10½ in), and glue and screw them to the insides of the legs, making sure that they fit snugly to the underside of the seat. Cut the hoof rails to 865 mm (2 ft 10 in), and round over the ends; you can also cut bevel edges on the central parts. With the hoof rails standing on their bottom edges, support the legs on pieces of 6 mm (¼ in) scrap wood, and mark and cut out the hoof notches in the hooves; mark the legs and hoof rails to ensure a good fit during assembly, then drill screw holes through the hooves.

5 Whether you turn the posts yourself or buy them ready-turned, mark and cut them to 330 mm (1 ft 1 in) length. Cut the top rail to 865 mm (2 ft 10 in), the bottom rail to 1054 mm (3 ft 5½ in), the cross-pieces to 406 mm (1 ft 4 in) and the bottom rail blocks to 75 mm (3 in). Glue and screw the cross-pieces to the underside of the bottom rail, and then drill a central 25 mm (1 in) dowel hole through both pieces. Glue and screw the bottom rail blocks to the ends of the underside of the bottom rail.

6 Drill 25 mm (1 in) dowel holes through the top rail, and matching holes 50 mm (2 in) deep into the tops and bottoms of the posts. Cut two dowels 100 mm (4 in) long, glue them into the bottom of the posts and glue and wedge them through the bottom rail and cross-pieces. Cut two dowels 75 mm (3 in) long, glue them into the top of the posts, and glue and wedge them through the top rail.

7 Mark and drill holes 150 mm (6 in) from each end of the hoof rails, pass the swing-irons through and fit washers over the ends.

293 mm
(11½ in)

145 mm (5 in)

150 mm (6 in)

267 mm
(10½ in)

45 mm
(1¾ in)

785 mm (2 ft 7 in)

150 mm (6 in)

125 mm
(5 in)

200 mm (8 in)

865 mm (2 ft 10 in)

330 mm (1 ft 1 in)

1054 mm (3 ft 5½ in)

560 mm (1 ft 10 in)

Leg

Hoof
rail

Scrap

Marking out
for hoof notch

TEMPLATES FOR HEAD,
LEGS AND BODY SIDES

Finishing and Decorating

Apply two or three coats of clear varnish, with a light rub-down between each coat. For the final touches, fix glass eyes into the socket holes with pine-coloured wood filler. (If the horse will be played with by children under 3 years do not use glass eyes or any other substitute as small objects are a choking hazard.) Glue simulated horsehair into the hole in the rump, and tap a small wedge underneath the tail for extra strength. To make the bridle and reins, cut strips of 10 mm (³/₈ in) red leather strapping to length and fix them to the head with 12 mm (¹/₂ in) brass roundhead screws.

8 Secure the swing-irons with split pins, check that the movement of the swing-irons is easy, then cover the split pins and washers with brass 'bowler hat' covers. Screw a steel strip to the top of the top rail, 75 mm (3 in) from each end, for the swing-irons to rest on. Drill screw and bolt holes for the swing-iron brackets. Smear a dab of grease onto the steel strips.

9 Place the tops of the swing-irons on the steel strips. Screw and bolt using a gripping washer to secure the nut the top brackets over them, ensuring that the swing-irons swing freely.

10 Lift the horse onto the hoof rails, and screw the hooves to the hoof rails. Cut the foot rest to 460 mm (1 ft 6 in), round the corners, and screw it crossways onto the hoof rails.

LIST OF MATERIALS *(measurements indicate cut size)*		
ITEM	SECTION	LENGTH
HORSE		
Softwood for head, 1	293 x 35 mm (11½ x 1⅜ in)	356 mm (1 ft 2 in)
Softwood for seat, 1	145 x 45 mm (5¾ x 1¾ in)	535 mm (1 ft 9 in)
Softwood for handle, 1	9 mm (¾ in) diameter	200 mm (8 in)
Softwood for rump, 1	45 x 35 mm (1¾ x 1⅜ in)	125 mm (5 in)
Softwood for seat back, 1	100 x 25 mm (4 x 1 in)	125 mm (5 in)
Softwood for legs, 4	150 x 21 mm (6 x ⅞ in)	1840 mm (6 ft)
Softwood for leg blocks, 2	115 x 35 mm (4½ x 1⅜ in)	255 mm (10 in)
Plywood for body sides, 2	100 x 10 mm (4 x ⅜ in)	535 mm (1 ft 9 in)
Softwood for hoof rails, 2, and foot rest, 1	45 x 19 mm (1¾ x ¾ in)	2190 mm (7 ft 2 in)
STAND		
Softwood for posts, 2	75 mm (3 in) diameter	660 mm (2 ft 2 in)
Softwood for top rail, 1, bottom rail, 1, bottom rail blocks, 2, and cross-pieces, 2	100 x 25 mm (4 x 1 in)	2679 mm (8 ft 9½ in)
Hardwood dowels, 4	25 mm (1 in) diameter	356 mm (1 ft 2 in)
Eyes, 2, bridle and reins, 1, and tail, 1		
Steel strips, 2, steel swing-irons, 2		
Brackets, 2, bolts, 2, washers, 2		
Split pins, 2, and brass covers, 4		
Woodscrews		

PLAYHOUSE

This attractive playhouse can be adapted to any dimensions to suit your garden or yard.
The size of the house is slightly larger than the base, to allow moisture to drip off it. The building
uses no joints in its construction, but is screwed and nailed together; the balcony is simply glued.

Baseboard

Pencil guidelines

1 Use the base board to mark out in full size the lengths of each of the frame components, including the four corner posts; if you use only one face of the base, this can be turned over when assembling the playhouse. Start with the front and back frames, and check the angles are correct.

2 Cut the frame components to length; where duplicate pieces are used in each end, cut double the amount. Fit each component into place, checking that you have cut the dimensions correctly according to the layout on the base board.

3 Clamp a couple of components to the base board, drill pilot holes, apply glue liberally and screw the components together – hand pressure should hold the joints until the screws hold them. Be careful not to overtighten the joints, because most of them go into end grain. Repeat the process for the two side frames, including the window braces.

4 Cut all the weatherboard cladding to length, aiming to use complete boards wherever possible. Position the first piece of weatherboard to the bottom of the frame, and nail it along the bottom edge and the top onto each piece of vertical framing. Add the other pieces of weatherboard, working from the bottom up and allowing a 25 mm (1 in) overlap on each one, and nailing only along the top edge into the verticals. Cut and nail the boards in place on all four sides of the frame. Cross-cut the timber for the door and window linings to length, and nail into place.

5 Cut the bearers to length from pressure-treated softwood. Mark out the positions on the bottom side of the baseboard (the side used for marking out the frames), and drill six holes per bearer up through with a 5 mm ($\frac{1}{16}$ in) bit; support the other side to prevent breakout. Turn over the board and countersink the holes. Apply glue to the bearers, clamp in place and screw as shown. Treat the bearers and both sides of the base with preservative, and leave to dry.

6 Clamp the corner posts to the ends, allowing them to protrude a little past the cladding, and drill pilot holes and screw into place. You will probably need an assistant to help you with this; once the end frames are joined by one side frame, the assembly can be held with extended sash cramps. Check for square at all stages of assembly.

7 Cut the ridge board to length and drop it into place at the top of the end frames. Cut two internal and two external fillets to length. Cut the chipboard for the roof panels slightly oversize, then place the first panel on the pitch of the roof, overhanging the back edge by 19 mm ($\frac{3}{4}$ in), and pin into place without driving the nails home. Position and pin the second roof panel.

8 Hold the internal angled fillets in place and mark a pencil line along the outside. Drill up for fixing screws, countersink the holes from above, apply glue and screw into place. Follow the same procedure for the two outer angled fillets. When in place, trim back the roof panels to finish flush with the outer fillets (see inset).

9 Cut the bearers for the underside of the roof – these fit on the inside and outside of each end, and at the end of the overhanging roof portion. Cut the angles to fit snugly, countersink from above, and glue and screw into place. Use offcuts of roofing felt to pack out the bearers that run up the insides before final fixing.

1702 mm (5 ft 7 in)

800 mm (2 ft 7½ in)

270 mm (10⅝ in)

340 mm (1 ft 1⅜ in)

1460 mm (4 ft 9½ in)

2356 mm (7 ft 8¾ in)

5 ft 11 in (1800 mm)

2388 mm (7 ft 10 in)

1702 mm (5 ft 7 in)

465 mm (1 ft 6¼ in)

1371 mm (4 ft 6 in)

598 mm (1 ft 11½ in)

760 mm (2 ft 6 in)

100 mm (4 in)

510 mm (1 ft 8 in)

311 mm (1 ft ¼ in)

457 mm (1 ft 5⅞ in)

523 mm (1 ft 8⅝ in)

400 mm (1 ft 3¾ in)

4 x shorter bearers

300 mm (11¾ in)

880 mm (2 ft 10¾ in)

2400 mm (8 ft)

2 x end bearers – full width

1460 mm (4 ft 9½ in)

Clamped
bargeboards

10 Cut the mineralized felt oversize, and tack it in place along the sides of the roof. Cut and mitre two sets of barge boards and apex moulding, if desired, then mark decorations along the bottom edges and cut them out with a jigsaw. Tack the felt under the ends of the roof and screw the barge boards to the roof trusses over the ends of the roof.

11 Cut the corner posts, rails and uprights for the balcony to length. Apply glue to the butt joints, and clamp until the glue sets – make sure that the gaps between the uprights are no more than 100 mm (4 in) apart, so that children's heads cannot get stuck in the gaps.

12 Mitre-cut some beading and use it as a rebate for the clear sheeting in the door and window frames. Trim the sheeting to size, and hold it in place with more mitre-cut beading.

13 If you want to put a window in the top ready-made louvre door, cut through the louvres and discard the wood. Cut the tongue off the remaining louvre, and line out the hole with glued and pinned timber. Use mitre-cut beading as for the other windows to hold the clear sheeting in position. Fit the doors to the frame with flush hinges, and a doorknob and roller catch on each door.

LIST OF MATERIALS *(measurements indicate cut size)*		
ITEM	SECTION	LENGTH
Plywood for base, 1	1220 x 12 mm (4 ft x ½ in)	2440 mm (8 ft)
Pressure-treated softwood for base bearers, 4	50 x 47 mm (2 x 1⅞ in)	9760 mm (32 ft)
Softwood weatherboard for cladding, 60	150 x 25 mm (6 x 1 in)	62.62 m (205 ft 5½ in)
Top louvre door, 1, and bottom louvre door, 1	460 x 45 mm (1 ft 6 in x 1¾ in)	1371 mm (4 ft 6 in)
Softwood for door knobs, 2		47 mm (1⅞ in) diameter
FRAME		
Softwood for verticals, 22, and horizontals (including window braces), 17	45 x 45 mm (1¾ x 1¾ in)	41.31 m (136 ft 9 in)
Softwood for door and window linings, 11	70 x 19 mm (2¾ x ¾ in)	5487 mm (17 ft 11¾ in)
Softwood for corner posts, 4	70 x 70 mm (2¾ x 2¾ in)	6120 mm (20 ft)
ROOF		
Chipboard for roof panels, 2	800 x 12 mm (2 ft 7½ in x ½ in)	4712 mm (15 ft 5½ in)
Softwood for roof ridge, 1, and underside bearers, 2	70 x 19 mm (2¾ x ¾ in)	5820 mm (19 ft 1¾ in)
Softwood for underside bearers, 10, and fillets, 4	45 x 19 mm (1¾ x ¾ in)	15.24 m (50 ft)
Softwood for barge boards/fascias, 2	125 x 19 mm (5 x ¾ in)	1730 mm (5 ft 8 in)
BALCONY		
Softwood for end posts, 4	45 x 45 mm (1¾ x 1¾ in)	2040 mm (6 ft 8 in)
Softwood for rails, 8, and uprights, 16	35 x 35 mm (1⅜ x 1⅜ in)	9736 mm (31 ft 11½ in)
Mineralized roofing felt, galvanized felt nails		
Clear sheeting and beading for windows		
Galvanized cabin hook		
Flush hinges, 4, roller door catches, 2		
Woodscrews, nails, chipboard screws		
Oval bright wire nails		

TOY TRUCK

*This sturdy six-wheeler truck features
a shape-sorter box and four shapes for younger
children. For children under 3 years,
the dimensions of the shapes must be increased
for safety purposes. The box can be removed
for older children, or a piece of plywood
can be fitted onto the sorter-box top.*

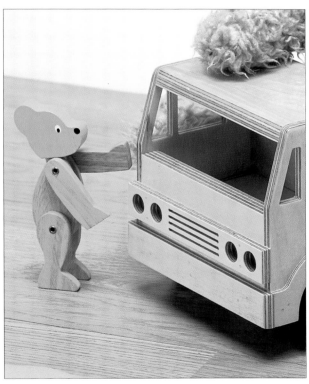

The cab front is nailed to the chassis.

295 mm (11⅝ in)

5-mm (³⁄₁₆-in) diameter axle holes

1 Mark and cut the chassis top and sides to 295 mm (11⅝ in) length. Tape or pin the sides together, mark and drill the three 5-mm (³⁄₁₆-in) diameter axle holes through both, and mark and cut them to shape with a fretsaw. Glue and pin the sides to the top; check that the axle holes are in alignment by fitting lengths of axle rod through the holes and placing a wheel onto each end. Rest the chassis on a flat surface and check that all the wheels are in contact with the surface.

2 Cut the cab front to 120 mm (4¾ in) length, and glue and pin it to the front of the chassis. Mark the cab sides to 115 mm (4½ in) length and cut them to shape with a fretsaw; don't remove the wheel arch shapes yet. Mark the wheel arches to 90 mm (3½ in) and cut them to shape with a fretsaw. Glue the wheel arches to the cab sides, holding them in place temporarily with pins. When the arches are set, cut out the arch shapes on the sides with a fretsaw.

3 Pin and glue the cab sides to the chassis and cab front. Cut the cab back and cab roof to 120 mm (4¾ in), and pin and glue them into position. To finish the cab, use a block plane to shape the front edge of the roof to make a smooth join. Mark and cut the front bumper to 140 mm (5½ in) and the lights/radiator section to 133 mm (5¼ in). On the lights/radiator, drill four 12-mm (½-in) diameter holes for the lights, and cut out four 2 mm (³⁄₃₂ in) slots 50 mm (2 in) long for the radiator grille. Glue and pin the front bumper to the front of the chassis, then position the lights/radiator 5 mm (³⁄₁₆ in) above it and glue and pin into position.

4 Cut the tailgate to 140 mm (5½ in) length, and shape with a fretsaw. Using a fretsaw, cut the 98 x 16 mm (3⅞ x ⅝ in) hole 8 mm (⁵⁄₁₆ in) above the bottom edge of the tailgate. Cut the flatbed to 225 mm (8⅞ in), position it on the chassis sides so that it overlaps them equally, and glue and pin in place. Position the tailgate to meet the bottom of the flatbed, and glue and pin in place. Smooth round the edges with abrasive paper, a rasp or file.

19 mm (³/₄ in)

219 mm (8⁵/₈ in)

40 mm (1⁵/₈ in)

25 mm (1 in)

30 mm (1¹/₈ in)

133 mm (5¹/₄ in)

50 mm (2 in)

110 mm (4¹/₄ in)

40 mm (1⁵/₈ in)

40 mm (1⁵/₈ in)

45 mm (1³/₄ in)

110 mm (4¹/₄ in)

98 mm (3⁷/₈ in)

6 mm (¹/₄ in)

4¹/₄ in (120 mm)

9 mm (⁵/₁₆ in)

90 mm (3¹/₂ in)

12 mm (¹/₂ in)

12 mm (¹/₂ in)

225 mm (8⁷/₈ in)

110 mm (4¹/₄ in)

12 mm (¹/₂ in)

32 mm (1¹/₄ in)

140 mm (5¹/₂ in)

115 mm (4¹/₂ in)

67 mm (2⁵/₈ in)

16 mm (⁵/₈ in)

133 mm (5¹/₄ in)

40 mm (1⁵/₈ in)

19 mm (³/₄ in)

50 mm (2 in)

45 mm (1³/₄ in)

35 mm (1⁵/₈ in)

30 mm (1¹/₄ in)

9 mm (⁵/₁₆ in)

21 mm (⁷/₈ in)

21 mm (⁷/₈ in)

62 mm (2¹/₂ in)

6 mm (¹/₄ in)

14 mm (⁹/₁₆ in)

140 mm (5¹/₂ in)

21 mm (⁷/₈ in)in

25 mm (1 in)

45 mm (1³/₄ in)

45°

10 mm (³/₈ in)

10 mm (³/₈ in)

6 mm (¹/₄ in)

110 mm (4¹/₂ in)

4 mm (¹/₈ in)

60 mm (2³/₈ in)

10 mm (³/₈ in)

165 mm (6¹/₂ in)

295 mm (11⁵/₈ in)

25 mm (1 in)

19 mm (³/₄ in)

5 Cut out the cube, square, rectangle and triangle to the sizes given in the list of materials (see opposite). Cut out each of the shapes and then smooth and round the edges. You can use a different coloured hardwood for each shape, as here, or make all four from the same wood and paint them later.

6 Mark and cut the shape sorter box front and back to 110 mm ($4\frac{1}{4}$ in) and the sides and base to 219 mm ($8\frac{5}{8}$ in). Plane all the meeting edges square and assemble with glue and pins. Mark and cut the shape sorter box top to 219 mm ($8\frac{5}{8}$ in). Mark the profiles of the shapes a fraction larger than the shapes themselves, so that they fit through easily. Cut out the shapes with a fretsaw, clean up the edges, then glue and pin the top to the box (see inset) and round all the edges with abrasive paper.

7 Drill four 9-mm ($\frac{5}{16}$-in) diameter dowel holes to a depth of 6 mm ($\frac{1}{4}$ in) in the base of the box. Fit with dowel markers and use to mark matching holes in the top of the flatbed, then drill dowel holes to 6 mm ($\frac{1}{4}$ in) depth. Cut four dowels to 12 mm ($\frac{1}{2}$ in) length, and glue into the holes in the box base.

8 Cut three axles to length and tap a spring hubcap on one end of each axle as shown. Put a wheel and then a washer onto the axles, and pass axles through one set of axle holes. Fit a washer and wheel to the other end of each axle, then tap on a spring hubcap to secure.

LIST OF MATERIALS (measurements indicate cut size)

ITEM	SECTION	LENGTH
TRUCK		
Birch plywood for chassis top, 1	110 x 12 mm ($4\frac{1}{4}$ x $\frac{1}{2}$ in)	295 mm ($11\frac{5}{8}$ in)
Birch plywood for chassis sides, 2	45 x 6 mm ($1\frac{3}{4}$ x $\frac{1}{4}$ in)	590 mm (1 ft $11\frac{1}{4}$ in)
Birch plywood for cab front, 1	65 x 12 mm ($2\frac{1}{2}$ x $\frac{1}{2}$ in)	120 mm ($4\frac{3}{4}$ in)
Birch plywood for cab sides, 2	90 x 6 mm ($3\frac{1}{2}$ x $\frac{1}{4}$ in)	230 mm (9 in)
Birch plywood for cab back, 1	67 x 12 mm ($2\frac{5}{8}$ x $\frac{1}{2}$ in)	120 mm ($4\frac{3}{4}$ in)
Birch plywood for cab roof, 1	80 x 10 mm ($3\frac{1}{8}$ x $\frac{3}{8}$ in)	120 mm ($4\frac{3}{4}$ in)
Birch plywood for wheel arches, 2	42 x 4 mm ($1\frac{11}{16}$ x $\frac{1}{8}$ in)	178 mm (7 in)
Birch plywood for front bumper, 1, and lights/radiator, 1	21 x 6 mm ($\frac{7}{8}$ x $\frac{1}{4}$ in)	273 mm ($10\frac{3}{4}$ in)
Birch plywood for tailgate, 1	40 x 6 mm ($1\frac{5}{8}$ x $\frac{1}{4}$ in)	140 mm ($5\frac{1}{2}$ in)
Birch plywood for flatbed, 1	150 x 6 mm (6 x $\frac{1}{4}$ in)	225 mm ($8\frac{7}{8}$ in)
SHAPE SORTER BOX		
Birch plywood for base, 1, and sides, 2	110 x 12 mm ($4\frac{1}{4}$ x $\frac{1}{2}$ in)	657 mm (2 ft $1\frac{7}{8}$ in)
Birch plywood for back, 1	45 x 12 mm ($1\frac{3}{4}$ x $\frac{1}{2}$ in)	110 mm ($4\frac{1}{4}$ in)
Birch plywood for front, 1	98 x 12 mm ($3\frac{7}{8}$ x $\frac{1}{2}$ in)	110 mm ($4\frac{1}{4}$ in)
Birch plywood for top, 1	133 x 6 mm ($5\frac{1}{4}$ x $\frac{1}{4}$ in)	219 mm ($8\frac{5}{8}$ in)
SHAPES AND WHEELS		
Ramin dowel for cylinder, 1	25 mm (1 in) diameter	50 mm (2 in)
Mahogany for triangle, 1	40 x 40 mm ($1\frac{5}{8}$ x $1\frac{5}{8}$ in)	50 mm (2 in)
Beech for cube, 1	30 x 30 mm ($1\frac{1}{8}$ x $1\frac{1}{8}$ in)	30 mm ($1\frac{1}{8}$ in)
Oak for rectangle, 1	40 x 19 mm ($1\frac{5}{8}$ x $\frac{3}{4}$ in)	50 mm (2 in)
Hardwood dowels, 4	9 mm ($\frac{5}{16}$ in) diameter	
Axles, 3, plastic wheels, 6	5 mm ($\frac{3}{16}$ in) diameter	
Spring hubcaps, 6	50 mm (2 in) diameter	
Moulding pins	19 mm and 25 mm ($\frac{3}{4}$ and 1 in)	

TEDDY BEAR BOOK ENDS

*These teddy bear book ends provide a decorative
way of keeping books neatly on a surface or shelf.
They are easy to construct, using dowel joints
and screwed butt joints, and can be made
with softwood and plywood offcuts.*

The profiles are cut out with a fretsaw.

1 You can either photocopy the two teddy bear shapes and enlarge them to the correct dimensions, or draw them freehand. Here, each bear is drawn separately on paper to 160 mm (6¼ in). Cut out the shapes and glue them onto 4 mm (⅛ in) birch plywood as shown.

2 Carefully cut around the character shapes using a powered fretsaw or hand fretsaw. With abrasive paper wrapped around a sanding block, sand off the paper and smooth the surfaces. Next, neaten all the edges by working around them with abrasive paper or a small file.

3 Mark and cut the two softwood bases to 140 mm (5½ in), and the two uprights to 200 mm (8 in) length. Leave the corners square, or mark corner curves and cut out using a fretsaw or jigsaw. In each base mark the two screw holes for the bears, then drill and countersink the pilot holes.

4 Cut six 25 mm (1 in) lengths from 6-mm (¼-in) diameter fluted hardwood dowelling. Mark the position for the three dowel holes on the meeting edge of each base. Attach a piece of sticky tape 12 mm (½ in) from the tip of a 6 mm (¼ in) drill bit, and drill the dowel holes to the depth shown by the sticky tape.

5 Insert brass dowel markers into the dowel holes, then position the base meeting edge to the face of the matching upright and press the two pieces together. Using the same marked drill bit, drill the dowel holes in the uprights. Glue and insert the dowels, then clamp the uprights and bases together and leave to dry.

6 Place each bear on its base, then push an awl or bradawl through the pilot screw holes to mark the hole positions on the bears' bottom edges. Drill pilot holes in the bears and screw each to its base. Undo screws, remove the bears and paint them using child-safe paints (see p. 72). Apply a finish to the bases and uprights. When dry, screw the bears to the bases.

160 mm (6¹/₄ in)

130 mm (5¹/₈ in)

125 mm (5 in)

200 mm (8 in)

30 mm (1¹/₈ in)

140 mm (5¹/₂ in)

19 mm (³/₄ in)

40 mm (1⁵/₈ in)

70 mm (2³/₄ in)

19 mm (³/₄ in)

LIST OF MATERIALS *(measurements indicate cut size)*

ITEM	SECTION	LENGTH
Birch plywood for teddy bears, 2	130 x 4 mm (5¹/₈ x ¹/₈ in)	320 mm (1 ft ¹/₂ in)
Softwood for uprights, 2, and bases, 2	125 x 19 mm (5 x ³/₄ in)	680 mm (2 ft 3 in)
Fluted hardwood dowels, 6	6 mm (¹/₄ in) diameter	150 mm (6 in)
No. 6 countersunk screws, 4	32 mm (1¹/₄ in)	
Baize, felt or sheet cork		
Brass dowel markers		

PINE BED

The basic frame of this versatile bed is sturdily constructed from softwood, using mortise-and-tenon joints and bed bolts, knock-down fittings that are easily assembled. You can vary the design and elaboration of the headboard and finials to add a personal touch.

You can turn the finials or buy them ready-made.

1 Mark and cut the boards for the headboard to slightly over 930 mm (3 ft ⅝ in), and for the footboard to slightly over 900 mm (2 ft 11¾ in). Plane the meeting edges square and cut for joining, using either a biscuit jointer and beech biscuits, dowels, or loose-tongue joints. Apply glue and clamp with sash cramps. When dry, check the boards for flat and trim to the finished lengths, checking for square.

2 Cut out a 12 mm (½ in) plywood template for the headboard top edge, then mark this on the headboard. Cut the top edge to shape. Use the same template to guide a router and decorative cutter for the moulding profile on the headboard's top edge. Add laminate to the template to bring it to 25 mm (1 in), then use a router guide to cut the same decorative groove on the face of the headboard, curved at the top and straight along the sides and bottom.

3 Next, sand the entire headboard piece using an orbital sander, and finish by carefully sanding along the grain by hand. Make sure that you smooth away any torn grain along the router cuts.

4 Cut a 12 mm (½ in) square notch at the top of the headboard sides to fit into the corner post mortises. Using a router, field the footboard edges to 12 mm (½ in), to fit into mortises in corner posts and end rails (see inset).

SIDE RAIL

CORNER
POST

145 mm
(5 3/4 in)

BED BOLT

600 mm (1 ft 11 5/8 in)

235 mm
(9 1/4 in)

570 mm
(1 ft 10 1/2 in)

150 mm
(6 in)

930 mm (3 ft 5/8 in)

850 mm (2 ft 9 3/4 in)

970 mm (3 ft 2 1/4 in)

267 mm
(10 1/2 in)

700 mm (2 ft 3 1/2 in)

930 mm
(3 ft 5/8 in)

1945 mm (6 ft 4 1/4 in)

267 mm (10 1/2 in)

Mark post ends to
identify positions

Finishing

*If you want to add variety when using pine or another
pale softwood, water-based stains are available in a wide
range of colours. Make sure that you stain and finish
the fielded edges of the footboard before fixing it dry*
*into position within the grooves of the end rails and corner
posts. This way, if the footboard shrinks, it will not
expose a white line of unfinished wood. Finish with
varnish or seal the wood before waxing it.*

5 Cut the head corner posts to 970 mm (3 ft 2¼ in) and the foot corner posts to 700 mm (2 ft 3½ in), and plane or sand the surfaces smooth. Make pencil marks on the posts to avoid confusion when marking out for jointing. Mark 100 x 25 mm (4 x 1 in) mortises starting 267 mm (10½ in) from the bottom of each corner post for the side rails, and chop out, using a mortise or bevel-edged chisel, or drill out waste wood and clean up with a chisel. Again starting 267 mm (10½ in) from the bottom of each corner post, cut out the 19 mm (¾ in) mortise for the headboard and the 12 mm (½ in) mortises for the footboard as shown.

6 Cut the end rails to 930 mm (3 ft ⅝ in), and cut 38 mm (1½ in) tenons flat on each end. Cut 12 mm (½ in) grooves for the footboard along the bottom edge of the top end rail and the top edge of the bottom end rail. At each end of the footboard mortises on the foot corner posts, chop out 38 mm (1½ in) mortises for the end rail tenons. Cut the side rails to 1945 mm (6 ft 4¼ in) and cut 100 mm (4 in) tenons on each end. Dry-assemble the entire frame, checking for square and making any adjustments, then mark matching components and disassemble.

7 Drill the holes for the bed bolts through the corner posts, using an electric drill and stand. Dry-assemble the corner posts and side rails, mark through the holes onto the side rail tenons and then hand-drill the bed bolt holes into the side rails. Carefully bore the recess for the nut in the inside face of the side rails, then make a trial fitting of the bed bolts and nuts, tightening until the shoulders of the rail tenons pull up square against the corner posts. Undo the bolts and disassemble.

8 Drill a 16 mm (⅝ in) dowel hole into the bottom of each finial. Mark the centre of the top of each corner post, and drill a matching dowel hole. Chamfer all the top and side edges of the corner posts, then glue in the dowels to the finials and post tops. Round over all sharp corners, using a router fitted with an ovolo cutter. Glue the head-board into the mortises in the head corner posts and clamp with sash cramps. Dry-fit the footboard into the grooves in the end rails, then glue up the end-rail tenons into the foot corner post mortises, and hold with sash cramps. Clean off surplus glue and leave to dry. Next, cut the slat rails to 1908 mm (6 ft 3⅛ in) and place along the side rails so the slats will be below the top edge; the height will be determined by the thickness of your mattress. Drill pilot holes and screw slat rails into place.

9 Assemble the frame and tighten the bed bolts. Cut the slats to 925 mm (3 ft $\frac{3}{8}$ in), and space evenly along the slat rails. Staple the slats to two lengths of webbing, then screw the head- and foot-end slats into place. Cut the head side panels to 600 mm (1 ft 11 $\frac{5}{8}$ in) and the foot side panels to 570 mm (1 ft 10$\frac{1}{2}$ in). Make a template for their shape, and cut with a jigsaw or bandsaw. Drill three dowel holes in the bottom edge and matching holes in the top edge of the side rails, and two pilot holes for each panel through the corner posts. Glue in the dowels and glue and screw the panels to the side rails and corner posts. Make rounded pegs and fit into the countersunk screw holes, to hide the screw heads.

LIST OF MATERIALS *(measurements indicate cut size)*

ITEM	SECTION	LENGTH
Softwood for head corner posts, 2, and foot corner posts, 2	65 x 65 mm (2$\frac{1}{2}$ x 2$\frac{1}{2}$ in)	3340 mm (10 ft 11$\frac{1}{2}$ in)
Softwood for side rails, 2	145 x 25 mm (5$\frac{3}{4}$ x 1 in)	3890 mm (12 ft 8$\frac{1}{2}$ in)
Softwood for slat rails, 2	45 x 25 mm (1$\frac{3}{4}$ x 1 in)	3816 mm (12 ft 6$\frac{1}{4}$ in)
Softwood for head side panels, 2, and foot side panels, 2	235 x 19 mm (9$\frac{1}{4}$ x $\frac{3}{4}$ in)	2340 mm (7 ft 8$\frac{1}{4}$ in)
Softwood for end rails, 2	75 x 45 mm (3 x 1$\frac{3}{4}$ in)	1860 mm (6 ft 1$\frac{1}{4}$ in)
Softwood for headboard, 1	830 x 19 mm (2 ft 8$\frac{3}{4}$ in x $\frac{3}{4}$ in)	930 mm (3 ft $\frac{5}{8}$ in)
Softwood for footboard, 1	267 x 19 mm (10$\frac{1}{2}$ x $\frac{3}{4}$ in)	908 mm (2 ft 11$\frac{3}{4}$ in)
Softwood for slats, 14	90 x 16 mm (3$\frac{1}{2}$ x $\frac{5}{8}$ in)	12.95 m (42 ft 5$\frac{1}{4}$ in)
Softwood for finials, 4	50 x 50 mm (2 x 2 in)	600 mm (2 ft)
Dowels, 12 and 4 respectively	10 mm ($\frac{3}{8}$ in), 16 mm ($\frac{5}{8}$ in) diameter	
Bed bolts, 4, wooden pegs, 12		
Beech biscuits, woodscrews, webbing		

STORAGE SHELVES

This simple shelving unit is easy to make, as there are no joints in its construction.
Using melamine-faced chipboard offers strength and a choice of finishes,
from pine or ash to a variety of colours.

1 Mark the sides to 1840 mm (6 ft) length and the shelves, top and kickboard to 770 mm (2 ft 6⅜ in) length. Score all the cutting lines heavily, to prevent breakout, and cut all the parts to size, using a power saw or by hand. Cut matching edging tape to size and iron it onto any exposed cut edges.

2 Apart from the top and the bottom shelf, which is placed 75 mm (3 in) from the bottom edge, the other five shelves can be positioned according to your particular requirements. Mark and drill two screw holes per shelf and top, set 50 mm (2 in) in from the front and back of the sides, and one screw hole each side for the kickboard, 50 mm (2 in) from the front.

3 Because ordinary woodscrews do not provide enough grip in chipboard, especially on such a large unit, use purpose-made 50-mm (2-in) long chipboard screws that have wide threads. Stand one of the sides on its edge and screw the top and shelves to it. Screw on the other side piece and tighten all the screws, checking for square, then add the kickboard in the same way.

4 Press screw cappings onto the screw heads, to disguise them. Wood-finish melamine looks best with matching cappings, but if you use coloured, black or white melamine, contrasting cappings can also look good.

5 Cut the melamine-faced hardboard for the back to size, then pin it to the back of the unit, spacing the pins at approximately 200 mm (8 in) intervals; again, you can use matching or contrasting colours.

LIST OF MATERIALS *(measurements indicate cut size)*		
ITEM	SECTION	LENGTH
Melamine-faced chipboard for sides, 2	356 x 14 mm (1 ft 2 in x $^9/_{16}$ in)	3680 mm (12 ft)
Melamine-faced chipboard for shelves, 6	350 x 14 mm (1 ft 1$^3/_4$ in x $^9/_{16}$ in)	4620 mm (15 ft 2$^1/_4$ in)
Melamine-faced chipboard for top, 1	356 x 14 mm (1 ft 2 in x $^9/_{16}$ in)	770 mm (2 ft 6$^3/_8$ in)
Melamine-faced chipboard for kickboard, 1	75 x 14 mm (3 x $^9/_{16}$ in)	770 mm (2 ft 6$^3/_8$ in)
Melamine-faced hardboard for back, 1	785 x 6 mm (2 ft 7 in x $^1/_4$ in)	1840 mm (6 ft)
Chipboard screws and cappings, 30	50 mm (2 in)	
Panel pins	25 mm (1 in)	
Edging tape		

356 mm (1 ft 2 in)

770 mm (2 ft 6⅜ in)

1840 mm (6 ft)

6 mm (¼ in)

75 mm (3 in)

Using Chipboard

Some of the advantages of using chipboard are that it is a light and inexpensive material and, when faced with any of a large range of melamine or hardboard veneers, easy to clean. In addition, it does not need to be finished or maintained. It is widely available in different widths and thicknesses, and is a standard material for kitchen and bedroom fittings. However, it does not take ordnary woodscrews well, so you have to use special chipboard ones, and once damaged, a piece cannot be repaired.

CHILD-SIZE TABLE SET

*This solid table and chair set is constructed
with biscuit joints. With careful planning,
it can be made from a single
2440 x 1220 mm (8 x 4 ft) sheet
of 19 mm (³/₄ in) MDF – you will need
more for extra chairs.*

The seat hole is rounded using a router.

1 Mark out the components onto the MDF: the table front and back legs are 500 mm (1 ft 7⅝ in), the table side legs 470 mm (1 ft 6½ in), the chair front legs 300 mm (11¾ in) and the chair side legs 265 mm (10⅜ in). Draw the various radii with a template to 50 mm (2 in), except for the back of the chair seat, which is 21 mm (⅞ in) and the seat back hole, which is 60 mm (2⅜ in).

2 Cut all the components to length. Make all the major straight cuts with a circular saw, using a guide bearer to ensure accuracy. Make the internal cuts for the leg components with a jigsaw, and sand their internal edges.

3 Use a 10 mm (⅜ in) round-over bit on both sides of the internal edges. These can simply be rounded-over, or the bit can be set to form a rebate detail, as shown here.

4 Round over both top and bottom edges of the table top and chair seat. Don't rout any edge which will form an external corner – this is much easier to do after assembly.

5 Start the seat back hole with a spade bit, and cut out the rest of the hole with a jigsaw. Sand and then finish both sides of the hole using the router fitted with the round-over bit.

600 mm (1 ft 11⅝ in)

600 mm (1 ft 11⅝ in)

86 mm (3⅜ in)

550 mm (1 ft 8⅞ in)

300 mm (11¾ in)

60 mm (2⅜ in)

120 mm (4¾ in)

300 mm (11¾ in)

340 mm (1 ft 1⅜ in)

470 mm (1 ft 6½ in)

75 mm (3 in)

200 mm (8 in)

Corners rounded after assembly

500 mm (1 ft 7⅝ in)

75 mm (3 in)

700 mm (2 ft 3½ in)

70 mm (2¾ in)

550 mm (1 ft 1 in)

45 mm (1¾ in)

27 mm (1¹⁄₁₆ in)

265 mm (10⅞ in)

300 mm (11¾ in)

Corners rounded after assembly

Working with MDF and Finishing

Although MDF is a generally stable material, its dust is potentially carcinogenic, and so it is advisable to do all cutting, sanding and routing outdoors. When working indoors or outside, a good dust mask is essential – if you intend to work with MDF regularly, it is worth investing the extra money in purchasing a professional-quality respirator. To finish the table and chair, apply two coats of primer and then two or three coats of gloss child-safe toy paint (see p. 72) sanding between coats.

6 Rout the internal edges of the chair back legs, and rout the front external edge. This edge should only be routed to within 16 mm (⅝ in) of the top of the chair seat. Once again, leave the back edge to be routed after assembly. Plane smooth any rough edges, to ensure that all external corners will be true.

7 The legs are assembled with beech biscuits and glue. Cut the biscuit slots in the meeting edges of the components, allowing for three No. 10 biscuits on each joint. Apply glue and insert the biscuits.

8 When clamping up the leg assemblies with sash cramps, it is a good idea to ask a friend to help. Here, the table top is held onto the assembly so that its position can be marked.

9 When the leg assemblies are dry, cut small blocks of pine offcuts to 70 mm ($2^3/4$ in) and glue them into place. You can either leave them square or shape them to fit into the internal corners, as illustrated here. Round over all the external corners of the leg assemblies, then use woodscrews to attach the table top and chair seat to the wooden blocks. Cover the screw heads with filler and sand smooth.

LIST OF MATERIALS *(measurements indicate cut size)*

ITEM	SECTION	LENGTH
TABLE		
MDF for top, 1	600 x 19 mm (1 ft $11^5/8$ x $^3/4$ in)	600 mm (1 ft $11^5/8$ in)
MDF for front and back legs, 2, and side legs, 2	530 x 19 mm (1 ft $8^7/8$ x $^3/4$ in)	1940 mm (6 ft $4^1/4$ in)
CHAIR		
MDF for seat, 1	340 x 19 mm (1 ft $1^3/8$ x $^3/4$ in)	300 mm ($11^3/4$ in)
MDF for front legs, 1, and side legs, 2	330 x 19 mm (1 ft 1 x $^3/4$ in)	830 mm (2 ft $8^1/2$ in)
MDF for back, 1	700 x 19 mm (2 ft $3^1/2$ x $^3/4$ in)	300 mm ($11^3/4$ in)
Pine for corner blocks, 8	70 x 16 mm ($2^3/4$ x $^5/8$ in)	560 mm (1 ft 10 in)
No. 8 woodscrews	38 mm ($1^1/2$ in)	
No. 10 beech biscuits		

TOY BOX

This useful and easily constructed toy storage box uses only butt joints, glued and pinned together, with some decorative moulding to provide visual interest. The carcass and lift-off lid use MDF, a stable and inexpensive material.

1 Using a T-square for accuracy, mark the carcass front and back to 760 mm (2 ft 6 in) length, the sides to 457 mm (1 ft 5⅞ in), and the base to 737 mm (2 ft 5 in). Score along the lines with a craft knife, to help the saw follow the lines accurately.

2 Cut the MDF to the correct dimensions using a hand saw – this produces less dust flying about the workshop than a power saw. Clean up the edges, ensuring that they are all square and flat.

3 Working from the base as a guide, glue and assemble the base, sides, front and back. Clamp up the carcass, and check that the right angles are accurate. To secure the joints further, drill pilot holes for panel pins along the edges, and hammer in the pins.

4 The joints for the front, back and sides can be given additional strength by cutting strips of quadrant section softwood to length and gluing them into the four inside corners. Make sure that the top of each strip is flush with the top of the carcass.

5 Measure and cut the chamfered softwood moulding for the corner joints around the base to length, using a mitre block or mitre saw.

6 Apply glue to the chamfered moulding and press it into position around the base, making sure that the mitred joints fit well together. For added strength, drill pilot holes and drive pins through the moulding.

7 Mark, score and cut the lid to 760 mm (2 ft 6 in) length, and clean up the edges. Measure and mitre-cut the half-round soft-wood moulding for the lid edges. Apply glue and place the moulding in position, holding it with adhesive tape, then drill pilot holes and pin into place. Clean up the whole box to finish.

LIST OF MATERIALS *(measurements indicate cut size)*		
ITEM	**SECTION**	**LENGTH**
MDF for front and back, 2, sides, 2, and base, 1	457 x 12 mm (1 ft 5⅞ in x ½ in)	3171 mm (10 ft 4¾ in)
MDF for lid, 1	485 x 12 mm (1 ft 7 in x ½ in)	760 mm (2 ft 6 in)
Softwood for corner strings	12 mm (½ in) quadrant section	1764 mm (5 ft 9½ in)
Softwood half-moulding for lid	12 mm (½ in) diameter	1730 mm (5 ft 8¼ in)
Softwood chamfered moulding for base	47 x 16 mm (1⅞ x ⅝ in)	2595 mm (8 ft 6⅛ in)
Panel pins		

485 mm (1 ft 7 in)

760 mm (2 ft 6 in)

12 mm (⅛ in)

457 mm (1 ft 5⅞)

457 mm (1 ft 5⅞)

457 mm
(1 ft 5⅞)

760 mm
(2 ft 6 in)

760 mm (2 ft 6 in)

Finishing and Decorating

The relatively characterless surface of MDF makes it a good vehicle for paint finishes after you have filled any gaps and to cover the pinholes, although you can stain it or even consider practising graining or combing techniques. Using non-toxic paints (see p. 72), you can paint it to match the decor of the child's room or go in for bold, colourful contrasts. Stencilling or hand-lettering are popular alternatives, particularly if you personalize a project with a child's name. Alternatively, you could apply cut-out decorations and then varnish over the whole box.

DRAWING EASEL

*This easel combines a chalking board on one side with a panel on the other,
for clipping paper for drawing or painting. The frames are constructed using
T-lap joints, and the shelf stops hold the frames in the correct open position.*

1 Mark and cut the four vertical
frame components to 1220 mm
(4 ft) and the four horizontals to
535 mm (1 ft 9 in). Mark the lap
part of the T-lap joints on the ends
of the horizontals, and the matching
recesses on the verticals. Cut the
joints, using a tenon saw and mitre
block for accuracy, then clean up
the waste in the recess.

2 Glue and clamp up the frame
components, making sure that
the verticals and horizontals are
parallel with each other. To assist
this, cut the boards to 610 mm (2 ft)
and clamp them in place temporarily
while the glue dries.

3 Set a sliding bevel to 45° and use
it to mark the angles for the four
corner triangles, then cut them
to 100 mm (4 in).

4 Use abrasive paper and a sanding block to round over
the edges of the triangles and the two boards, starting
with a medium-grade and finishing with a fine-grade
abrasive paper. Check the width between the frame
verticals, and cut the shelf to 610 mm (2 ft) length.

5 Mitre-cut the half-round beading to fit along
the top edges of the shelf, and glue it in place;
you can reinforce it with small pins. Glue the triangles
in place on the top corners of the frames, and glue
the boards in position, again reinforcing with pins.

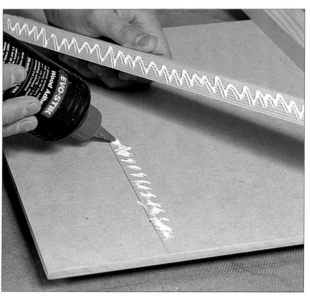

6 Lay the completed frames on a flat surface with their top edges touching, screw the flap hinges into place, and stand the easel upright. Cut the shelf stops to 430 mm (1 ft 5 in) and use a sliding bevel to calculate the slope to be chamfered on them. Use a plane to cut the chamfer.

7 Glue and clamp the stops parallel and equidistant on the underside of the shelf, ensuring that the chamfer makes the stops slope outwards to keep the easel from opening out too far. Drill pilot holes through the stops into the shelf, and reinforce the joint with screws.

LIST OF MATERIALS *(measurements indicate cut size)*		
ITEM	SECTION	LENGTH
Softwood for frame verticals, 4, frame horizontals, 4, and shelf stops, 2	50 x 25 mm (2 x 1 in)	7800 mm (25 ft 10 in)
MDF for boards, 2	510 x 9 mm (1 ft 8 in x $^5/_{16}$ in)	1220 mm (4 ft)
MDF for shelf, 1	430 x 9 mm (1 ft 5 in x $^5/_{16}$ in)	610 mm (2 ft)
MDF for triangles, 4	100 x 9 mm (4 x $^5/_{16}$ in)	400 mm (1 ft 4 in)
Half-round softwood beading	25 mm (1 in) wide	2080 mm (6 ft 10 in)
Brass flap hinges, 2	50 mm (2 in)	
Panel nails, woodscrews		

555 mm (1 ft 9 in)

1220 mm (4 ft)

610 mm (2 ft)

510 mm (1 ft 8 in)

267 mm (10½ in)

Finishing

Although you can paint and varnish the whole easel after final construction, it may be easier and more effective to finish the parts as you go along: apply clear or coloured varnish to the two frames after you have glued them up, and paint the MDF components – the triangles, boards and shelf – with child-safe paints before you glue them to the frames. You can paint the whole shelf in one colour after the beading has been attached, or you can paint the beading a contrasting colour.

CATERPILLAR PEG RAIL

This friendly caterpillar is an ideal storage solution for a child's bedroom or playroom – its three pegs can take clothes, toys, shoe bags and more. The body is cut out with a fretsaw, and the pegs and dowels can be bought ready-turned.

The nose screw secures the rail to the wall or door.

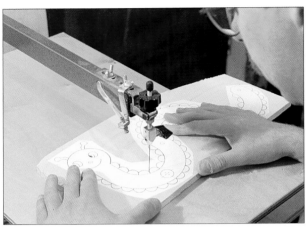

1 Either photocopy the diagram of the caterpillar (see right) and enlarge it to the correct dimensions, or you can draw it freehand onto paper. Cut out your drawing and then glue it onto a piece of 12 mm ($\frac{1}{2}$ in) MDF or birch plywood.

2 Use a powered or hand fretsaw to cut out the caterpillar profile, taking care to shape the curves consistently. Mark the positions of the fixing screws on the body, and drill clearance holes for No. 6 screws; the screw for the nose is a roundhead one, so countersink only the other three holes.

Completed pegs

Dowel hole

10 mm ($\frac{3}{8}$ in) diameter dowel

3 Mark and drill three 10 mm ($\frac{3}{8}$ in) holes in the caterpillar body for the pegs as shown. Wrap abrasive paper around a sanding block and then sand the guide drawing off the body, making sure that the surface is even. Smooth away any unevenness from the edges of the body, using abrasive paper and small files.

4 You can either turn a dowel rod to 10 mm ($\frac{3}{8}$ in) diameter, or purchase it ready-made. Sand it smooth and cut three 30 mm ($1\frac{1}{8}$ in) lengths from it. Again, the three 19-mm ($\frac{3}{4}$ in) diameter hardwood balls can be turned or purchased; drill a 10 mm ($\frac{3}{8}$ in) hole 6 mm ($\frac{1}{8}$ in) deep in each ball, and glue in a length of dowel. When it is completely dry, glue the pegs into the dowel holes in the body.

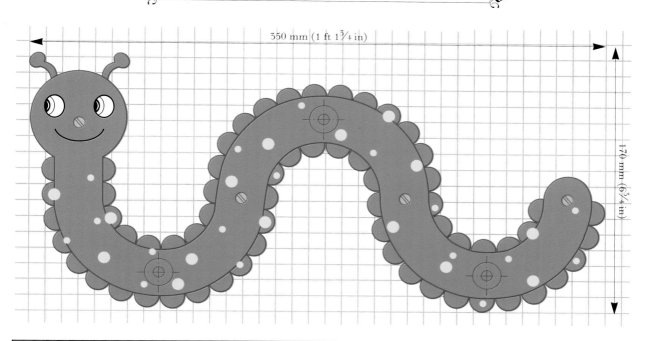

350 mm (1 ft 1¾ in)

170 mm (6¾ in)

LIST OF MATERIALS *(measurements indicate cut size)*		
ITEM	SECTION	LENGTH
MDF or birch plywood for body, 1	170 x 12 mm (6¾ x ½ in)	350 mm (1 ft 1¾ in)
Hardwood dowels, 3	10 mm (⅜ in) diameter	90 mm (3½ in)
Hardwood balls, 3	19 mm (¾ in) diameter	
No. 6 countersunk screws, 3		
No. 6 roundhead screw, 1		

Finishing and Fixing

You can paint or stain the caterpillar in any colours you choose, although green and yellow are probably the most obviously suitable – as always with objects for children's rooms, make sure that the finishing material you use is suitable for toys.

To fix the caterpillar, position it on a wall or door and mark and drill the holes. If you are fixing to a wall, insert wall plugs. Use the three countersunk screws for the body, and the roundhead screw for the nose – this can be painted when it is secure.

CHARACTER MOBILE

*This colourful mobile brightens up
any child's room, with its cloud hangers
and five flying characters cut out
from thin plywood. You can adapt
the theme to your child's favourite
characters, making sure that
you test them for balance first.*

Use a range of child-safe paints in primary colours.

1 Either photocopy the characters and enlarge them to the correct dimensions, or draw them freehand. Here, the bee is 75 x 60 mm (3 x 2⅜ in), the kite 98 x 67 mm (3⅞ x 2⅝ in), the butterfly 110 x 65 mm (4¼ x 2½ in), the bird 125 x 80 mm (5 x 3⅛ in) and the sun 125 x 125 mm (5 x 5 in). Cut out the shapes and glue them onto 4 mm (⅛ in) birch plywood.

2 Cut out the characters out using a powered or hand fretsaw, then drill a small hole as shown in each for the hanging thread – the thickness of the hole will depend on the thickness of the thread. Also drill a hole for the tail of the kite. Using abrasive paper around a sanding block, sand off the paper and smooth the surfaces, then go around the edges with abrasive paper or small files.

3 Either photocopy the two hangers and enlarge them to 330 mm (1 ft 1 in) length, or draw them freehand. Cut out the shapes and glue them to 6 mm (¼ in) MDF or birch plywood, then cut them out with a fretsaw. Sand and smooth the edges. Mark and cut the slots for the halving joint, and pare away any surplus waste wood with a sharp chisel, or file the slots to fit.

4 Drill a small hole at the ends of the hangers as shown, for the thread for the characters. Again, the thickness of the hole will depend on the thickness of the thread. Apply glue to the slots and assemble the hangers, making sure that they are at right angles to each other.

5 When completely dry, paint the hangers and the characters, using child-safe paints (see p. 72). Cut ribbon or shiny paper for the kite tail, and attach it. Screw the curtain eyelet to the top of the assembled hangers, and the small eyelet centrally to the underside.

Hanging the Mobile

First, cut lengths of strong thread for each character. Hang the characters from the hangers, with one depending from the central small eyelet. Screw a cup hook or a large eyelet to the ceiling, then cut the cord to the required length. Tie it to the ceiling eyelet and the curtain eyelet on top of the hangers.

75 mm (3 in)
60 mm (2³⁄₈ in)

162 mm (6³⁄₈ in)
55 mm (2¹⁄₄ in)
30 mm (1¹⁄₈ in)
330 mm (1 ft 1 in)
55 mm (2¹⁄₄ in)
30 mm (1¹⁄₈ in)
6 mm (¹⁄₄ in)
330 mm (1 ft 1 in)

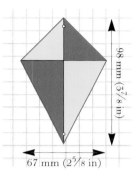

98 mm (3⁷⁄₈ in)
67 mm (2⁵⁄₈ in)

110 mm (4¹⁄₄ in)
65 mm (2¹⁄₂ in)

125 mm (5 in) square

80 mm (3¹⁄₈ in)
125 mm (5 in)

LIST OF MATERIALS *(measurements indicate cut size)*		
ITEM	SECTION	LENGTH
Birch plywood for characters, 5	125 x 4 mm (5 x ¹⁄₈ in)	400 mm (1 ft 3³⁄₄ in)
MDF or birch plywood for hangers, 2	55 x 6 mm (2¹⁄₄ x ¹⁄₄ in)	660 mm (2 ft 2 in)
Curtain eyelet, 1, and small brass eyelet, 1		
Thread, cord, and ribbon or shiny paper		

SAFE PAINTS AND STENCILLING

*The manufacture of 'child-safe' paints has been developed in response
to public demand for non-toxic coverings for children's toys and furniture.
The old art of stencilling is an ideal way to personalize an item for your child.*

Stencilling
*You can stencil with crayon, wax,
paint and stains. Work from
the outside in for an even effect.*

Safe paints
*Safe paints are non-toxic
and environmentally friendly.*

Safe Paints

When choosing paint for children's projects it is important to have a basic understanding of the contents of the paint you use to avoid bringing children into contact with potentially harmful substances.

Paint consists of pigments ground in binders, which form the paint film after the solvents in which the binders are dissolved have evaporated. The binder, also known as polymer, can be made from oils and resins and may be soluble in solvents such as white spirit; acrylic emulsion resins are dispersed in water.

Paint manufacturers are very aware of the possible harmful effects of their products, both to the person who applies the paint and to the person who uses the painted object – no paint produced for the UK domestic market now contains added lead, but there could be other traces of metals, and these could cause harm if a child were to suck or bite a toy or furniture that had been painted. Nearly all manufacturers' catalogues provide some information on the toxicity and safety of the products, and the paints themselves are, for the most part, clearly labelled. Although the majority of regulations were first produced for industry and for professional firms, they are there to help protect anyone who uses the products. For example, when finishing toys or furniture that may come in for some hard and sometimes unorthodox treatment, it is a wise move always to use the safest and most child-friendly materials possible.

There is, however, no single internationally recognized system of classification. As a result of this, different countries have different standards for child-safe paints and varnishes. In the UK, the British Standards Institute, working with the European Toy Safety Standards, sets out safety requirements. Always bear in mind that, if you are making toys that you intend to sell, you will need to obtain a certificate of conformity for the paint you use from the manufacturer.

In addition, some companies have also begun to respond to growing concern about the effect on the environment of chemical products and by-products. This awareness has given rise to use alternative methods of producing paint. In most cases, this has meant returning to traditional, natural ingredients, and manufacturers of such 'organic' paints are quick to point out that their products are safe for use on toys and children's furniture, and can be used by people who are sensitive or allergic to standard paints and finishes. An added advantage is that they do not seal the wood like modern gloss and emulsion paints, but rather allow it to 'breathe', thereby eliminating the problem of trapped moisture. However, these alternatives are still noticeably more expensive than regular paints, due to the cost of the natural ingredients and the smaller amounts that are currently produced, and they are not always easy to find. There are companies which specialize in these paints but manufacturers that produce standard paints are beginning to offer 'organic' ranges.

Preparing and Working with Paints

Whatever the paint you purchase, and whatever the various uses you intend to put it to, make sure that you follow the manufacturer's instructions – particularly where safety procedures are involved. For example, if you plan to spray paint onto a project, always make sure that you take adequate precautions – such as goggles or face mask, respirator, or disposable gloves. It makes absolutely no sense to spend time making a toy or piece of children's furniture and then to risk damaging your or the child's health, just for the sake of speed or an easy life.

If you need to remove old paint before repainting with paint that conforms to toy safety regulations, this should be removed carefully, because it may contain lead, and the resulting dust or flakes could give rise to the poisoning effects that lead produces. Children up to the age of five are at the greatest risk of contamination from the toxic side effects, one of these being impaired brain development, which can permanently impair mental functions.

To avoid contamination by dust, do not rub down old paint with sandpaper – this will only put lead-rich dust into the air and throughout the house. Either rub the old paint down using wet-and-dry sandpaper with water, or use a chemical paint stripper. Ideally, remove the old paint in an outdoor space to minimize the risk of dust contamination – always wear protective clothing while doing this. If you decide to use a hot-air gun, do this with great care, so as not to cause the paint to burn. Even though it may appear to be the quickest option, do not use a blow lamp, because this will create fumes when the paint is burnt. The paint that has been removed should be put into a sealed bag and placed in a household waste bin; it should not be burned.

It is important to remember that paints that comply with toy safety regulations are only safe when they are dry. While it is still in the liquid form, paint should be kept out of the reach of children; in addition, ensure that there is good ventilation in the room where it is being applied, and that you allow the paint to dry fully before using the toy or piece of furniture.

Stencil brushes
Stencil brushes have short bristles cut to give a flat edge for stippling and dabbing. Use non-toxic products at all times.

Repeating patterns
Make sure that you have worked out the meeting points or corners before you begin stencilling, to avoid overlaps or clashes.

Using a roller
For stencilling large areas or using repeated designs on a floor or on a wall, a roller can be useful, so long as you remove excess paint.

Checking the stencil
Whatever technique you use, it is vital to partly remove the stencil at one end or corner, to check that the effect is as you want it.

Stencil Brushes and Paints

Stencil brushes are produced specially for the purpose, and using other types of brushes just will not work. The stiff, short bristles are square-cut to give a flat edge that is designed for the stabbing action necessary for stencilling. Most brushes have metal ferrules, but some are intended for water work and are made without the ferrule. As with all brushes, it is advisable to buy the best that you can afford – cheap ones bought for the sake of economy will not last long, and brushes that are well looked after should continue to give good service for a long time. It is also possible to use small rollers for one-colour stencils.

Paints used for stencilling need to be fast-drying – special stencil paints are available, but the same results can be obtained from standard water-based acrylic paints. These can be used straight from the tin or jar, or you can mix your own colours. The essential point to remember is not to dilute the paint, otherwise it can creep under the stencil and ruin all your good work.

Making Stencils

There is a great variety of commercially produced stencils available, ranging from the simple to the complex; some can be purchased from art and craft stores, while others can be found in non-copyright books of stencil designs. However, there is no reason why you should not make your own stencils – perhaps to fit a particular piece of furniture – and once you get started, you will find the process of creating designs a fascinating one. Before photocopying printed designs or tracing them from other stencilled furniture, make sure that you are not infringing any copyright laws.

If you use stencilling card, just draw the design straight onto it and cut out the design carefully, using a sharp craft knife or scalpel. Alternatively, draw the design onto a piece of paper and use this as a template for a piece of clear acetate. Lightly tape the acetate over the template, and cut out the design with the knife or scalpel.

Applying the Paint

Before stencilling on a finished piece of woodwork, experiment on scrap wood, card or paper, so that you get a feel for stencilling. The best results are made on wood that has been sealed first, or on already painted surfaces. Tape the stencil in place on the wood – masking tape allows it to be lifted and repositioned easily – or use repositioning glue. If you intend to use the same stencil as a repeating motif, mark out the fixing positions before starting.

Whether you use a stencil brush or roller, the golden rule is to underload it with paint rather than overloading; you will find that surprisingly little is needed. Wipe or dab the bristles on scrap paper before you begin, to remove any excess paint. Use a stippling action through the stencil, working in from the cut edges; aim to produce an even covering, and be prepared to reload the brush at frequent intervals. As you go along, partly remove the stencil to check you are happy with the effect; replace it carefully and carry on. When you have finished, remove the stencil and allow the paint to dry fully. Because the layer of stencilled paint is quite fragile, it is a good idea to protect it with a layer or two of clear varnish.

Further Techniques

You can vary the depth of colour by applying more or less paint in required places, and by using stencils as a base for painting by hand – when the stencilled paint is dry, use fine artist's brushes to add details, shading or contrasts.

Although it is the standard medium, you don't have to use paint when stencilling – two other media are woodstains and coloured waxes. Water-based stains create a more transparent effect, where the grain of the wood can be seen under the colour. Make sure that the stencil is fixed to prevent any seeping under, and dab the brush on scrap paper after loading, to ensure that you have not overloaded it. Experiment with overlapping colours by adding a second colour on top of a first, using a clean brush for each colour.

A delicate sheen can be achieved by mixing pigments with neutral or clear wax. Use a stencil brush to mix the wax and coloured pigment, remove any excess from the bristles, and rub the brush onto the wood from the sides of the stencil, to avoid build-up. This technique looks particularly good with blended colours and simple designs – again, protect the finished stencil with clear varnish or shellac.

Using colours
You can experiment with using a number of different colours on the same stencil, and practice creating deeper or lighter shades for variety.

Using stains
The secret of successful decorating with stains is to make sure that you only have a little on the brush, and to begin with simple designs.

Stencilling with wax
Using pigments allows you to create subtle shades and to make delicate blends and overlaps.

INDEX

ACKNOWLEDGEMENTS

Makers

Peter Bishop: Playhouse (p. 24).

Mike Denley: Pine Bed (p. 40).

Anthony Dew: Rocking Horse (p. 16). (The Rocking Horse is based on an original design by Anthony Dew © 1990. Fittings to suit this horse are available from The Rocking Horse Shop, Fangfoss, York, Y041 5JH, England.)

Peter Dunsmore: Drawing Easel (p. 60).

Lester Haynes: Child-size Table Set (p. 50).

Jeff and Jennie Loader: Animal Safari (p. 10); Toy Truck (p. 30); Teddy Bear Book Ends (p. 36); Caterpillar Peg Rail (p. 64); Character Mobile (p. 68). (Jeff Loader designs and constructs toys, games and small items of decorative furniture. He undertakes commissions and may be contacted on 01458 834071.)

Les Meehan: Toy Box (p. 56, stencilled by Patricia Meehan).

Thanks also to Helen Adkins, Eric Kendall and Janet Swarbrick for their valued contribution.

Stylist

Claire Worthington: pp. 24, 30–31, 36–37, 50–51, 60, 64–65, 68–69

Photographers

Geoff Dann: pp. 24, 30–31, 36–37, 50–51, 60, 64–65, 68–69

Les Meehan: pp. 56–58.

Illustrators

All artworks by Keith Field, except the templates on pp. 13, 39, 67 and 71 which are the work of David Ashby.

Traditional Woodworking is Britain's leading monthly magazine for woodworkers, blending traditional style with the latest techniques. Each issue offers up to five projects for your workshop plus regular columns on wood finishing, furniture repair and restoration, as well as tests and news of all the latest hand and power tools. *Traditional Woodworking* is available through all good newsagents, but in case of difficulty, or to order a subscription, call the Reader Services Hotline on 01283 742970.